How to be a GHASTLY GRANDPARENT

...and have fun!

JASON THORNFALL

Crombie Jardine
PUBLISHING LIMITED

Office 2, 3 Edgar Buildings
George Street
Bath
BA1 2FJ
www.crombiejardine.com

Published by Crombie Jardine Publishing Limited
First edition, 2008
Copyright © Crombie Jardine Publishing Limited 2008

All rights are reserved. No part of this publication
may be reproduced, stored in a retrieval system, or
transmitted, in any form or by any means, electronic,
mechanical, photocopying, recording or otherwise,
without the prior written permission of the publisher.

ISBN 978-1-906051-19-8

Written by Jason Thornfall

Cover and text designed by www.glensaville.com

Printed in China

Contents

Introduction p.5

Looming Grandparenthood p.12

Grand Behaviour p.19

Grand Babies and Infants p.47

Grand Children p.65

Grand Teenagers p.86

Grand Adults p.101

Grand Decline p.108

Grand Exit p.119

And Finally p.123

Introduction

You've just completed at least two decades raising your offspring. Twenty years of patience-stretching tantrums, teenage mood swings, constant raids on your bank account, mind blowing pop music and 'I'm right, you're wrong' arguments. It seemed they'd never end.

From soiled nappies to moving into their first home... the tears of joy you shed at their wedding were a sign that you, at long

How to be a GHASTLY GRANDPARENT

last, had your life back. You were a free agent again. Let them do the worrying from now on, not you.

You've done your bit to keep the human race going and now you're looking forward to watching (from a distance) your children suffer the exact same traumas of married life as you did. You have a great deal of first hand experience... if they never took your advice before, why should they now?

Because they're about to start their own

...and have fun!

families, that's why. Take care, or you'll be roped in to share the pain. For another twenty years. At least. Will it ever end?

Will you have to wait until you're lying in your coffin to find the peace you've sought all your life? Or would you rather enjoy whatever time you have left? Doesn't take much thinking about, does it?

Before you suffer inevitable pangs of guilt, remember the resentment you felt when your own parents interfered with your life

How to be a GHASTLY GRANDPARENT

when you were expecting your first child? Frustrating, wasn't it? Always poking their noses in where they weren't wanted, buying incredibly large, brightly coloured plastic toys which lasted all of two minutes and generally spoiling their grandchildren to the point of making them uncontrollable, surly, selfish and thoroughly unbearable.

You certainly don't want to let your own new-to-parenthood children suffer the same way, do you? Or your grandchildren turn out to be spoiled brats like your own kids?

...and have fun!

You owe it to them to stand firm.

How will they learn without making their own mistakes and muddling through like the rest of mankind? There are no easy answers, and why should they keep running to you to sort out their problems? It's not fair for them to continue to expect unquestioning support from you. They've made their bed, so why should you lie in it? That's not to say you shouldn't give any help at all... quite the contrary, especially when they experience genuine disasters.

How to be a **GHASTLY GRANDPARENT**

But normal, day-to-day involvement must be given on your terms, not theirs.

This book contains guidance for a stress-free life for grandparents... everything you need to know to make you the absolute last resort when your children and grandchildren ask you to bail them out yet again.

Read it carefully. It will be your conduct guide for the rest of your life. Use it well and, should you feel the need, add your own notes to pass on your experience to future

...and have fun!

readers. Not only will you improve the quality of your own life, you'll provide an invaluable service to your descendants in particular and mankind in general.

Looming Grandparenthood

...and have fun!

Your first reaction to being told you're going to be a grandparent must be to express concern and assume the pregnancy wasn't planned. Make pointed observations, heavily sympathetic comments and polite enquiries, such as:

- *I told you too much red wine on a Saturday night would cause trouble.*

- *That's what comes of sitting in the office pregnancy chair.*

- *Didn't they tell you that having sex when*

How to be a GHASTLY GRANDPARENT

standing up was a sure way of not getting pregnant?

- *When was the last power cut?*

- *I can't understand why anyone would want to bring yet another child into a world torn apart by war, hunger and greed.*

- *How can you afford to raise a child and pay a mortgage?*

- *You'd better start saving for a family-sized car.*

- *Did you win the Lottery?*

...and have fun!

- *Those morning-after pills aren't 100% reliable, are they?*

- *Condom split, then?*

- *Who's the father?*

However, sympathy is one thing. Offering to help is another. Start as you mean to go on... in no circumstances say you'll buy baby clothes, bed linen, a cot, pram or anything else which will set a precedent or, more to the point, imply a willingness to get involved.

How to be a GHASTLY GRANDPARENT

Remember your own mother turning up with a rummage sale's worth of knitted baby jackets and her great-grandmother's moth-hole-ridden cream crocheted Christening shawl? Don't make the same mistake!

However, you should appear supportive. Give tactful practical gifts to the pregnant mum on her birthday or at Christmas... these should include personal essentials like indigestion tablets, nutmeg, ointment for piles and knitting needles (she'll have a lot of time on her hands as the Big Day

...and have fun!

approaches). Prospective fathers will welcome *Playboy* magazines and a tube of KY gel. Wrap them in highly noticeable paper and watch his wife's face when he rips it open. Priceless! Your consideration at such a traumatic time will undoubtedly be much appreciated. Their looks of embarrassment will be something to cherish and they may even regard you with more than a hint of respect. Or anxious suspicion... If you're capable of such outrageous behaviour before the child has even had its gender determined, what other surprises lie in store over the next few decades? Fear of the unknown is a wonderful weapon!

Grand Behaviour

How to be a GHASTLY GRANDPARENT

It's essential to your future welfare that you give serious consideration to changing your behaviour; at least until the last and youngest grandchild has reached adulthood. You may decide to continue that behaviour to the end of your days, so you must get it right.

Now that your children have their own offspring, they'll suddenly realise that you are (relatively speaking) old. Everything you do will be subject to their extremely perceptive scrutiny. They'll be looking for signs that you've 'lost it'. The response you

...and have fun!

gave earlier, when they announced the pregnancy, will have set alarm bells ringing but they'll have been so preoccupied with subsequent events that they won't have paid much attention to you or your funny little ways. On the other hand, their lives have now been turned upside down, their pleasures limited and the horrible truths of modern living will be sinking in fast.

This is where your cunning plans come in. You don't mind helping from time to time but you really do need to make sure you're

How to be a GHASTLY GRANDPARENT

not taken for granted. The way you behave from now on is critical.

Sit back for a moment and think about what appals you when you see folk older than yourself? And how can those quirks be adapted to suit your own needs?

Idiosyncrasies to bear in mind are:

Appearance

- *Threadbare scruffiness doesn't occur*

...and have fun!

naturally, it has to be cultivated. Don't throw away old handkerchiefs, clothes or shoes. Don't clean these things too often, and remember to wear them when frying onions as the smell will linger for days. Woollen jumpers, cardigans and sweaters are great smell-retainers.

- *At family events, wear shabby clothes in preference to the good attire you use when going out with friends.*

- *Walk with a stoop and develop a limp in damp weather. Rub your arm/shoulder/leg mysteriously from time to time.*

- *Appear vague, forgetful and generally just slightly bewildered.*

Personal Hygiene

- *Keep clean for your own health, but rely on subtle ploys to make it seem as though you're not looking after yourself. Don't wash your hair for a few days before attending a family gathering or important function, and do some last-minute gardening before you're due to leave; this will ensure that your finger*

...and have fun!

nails are noticeably dirty.

- *Keep a cat deterrent spray handy and give yourself a couple of squirts around the ankles... it smells awful and folk will think you have a deeply personal problem. Also, put a moth ball in at least one pocket. And take to eating raw garlic.*

- *Cultivate nasal, ear and (especially if you're a woman) chin hair. Use cheap aftershave and eau de toilette and heavily scented talc. Men should always leave traces of foam around their ears, and miss odd patches on their chin and upper lip when shaving.*

Penury

- *Constantly moan about the cost of living, inflation, Council tax, utility bills and maintenance contracts ('How am I supposed to buy food?').*

- *Keep loose change in a tatty leather flip-open wallet and never have a (screwed-up) note worth more than £5 in your pocket. Make it obvious you can't*

...and have fun!

afford fripperies. Never be embarrassed to borrow a tenner... and then conveniently forget to repay it. Often.

Drinking

- *Stale beer on the breath is preferable to stale whisky and can be acquired at lower cost. Elderly women should dab Gordon's gin behind their ears before meeting the family. Keep an empty hip flask and replenish it at your son or daughter's home when no one is looking.*

How to be a GHASTLY GRANDPARENT

Eating Habits

- *Dribbling convincingly is an art but easily over-played. So is chewing with your mouth open.*

- *Acquire a taste for unusual combinations, like jam and Gorgonzola sandwiches.*

- *When in family company, act as though you haven't had a decent meal for weeks.*

- *A little dried egg on the chin and down your front is a common sign of ageing.*

...and have fun!

Personal Emissions

- *Farting is a natural hazard; we all do it. Fortunately, people below a certain stage in their lives make every effort to control breaking wind, its volume and duration, often with limited success. In fact, your duty as a grandparent is to aspire to the opposite. Make it seem as though you're totally out of control.*

- *On the evening before a visit, eat fart-enhancing food: pizzas laced with eight garlic cloves, a large raw onion plus copious quantities of sprouts, cabbage, etc. are an absolute must. Baked beans on granary toast will suffice if fart preparation time is short: allow four hours for the whole thing to take full effect. Then bide your time.*

- *Discreet seeping emissions inside a crowded car on a warm day give best results and will create doubt as to whether you or your recently potty-trained grandchild are to blame. Other opportune moments occur when you are rising from the dining table or an armchair.*

...and have fun!

- *Obvious cheek-raising in full view, followed by a sound like strangled air coming from the squeezed neck of a balloon is guaranteed to cause extreme embarrassment to others, especially when outsiders (like the vicar) are also present. Farting while walking can be a joy and a mark of achievement, especially if you can emit a succession of short raspers in time with your step.*

- *Burping, belching ('better out than in') and a dribbling nose complete with bogies also have their part to play; exploit them to the full.*

How to be a GHASTLY GRANDPARENT

Communication

- *Grumble and grunt or, better still, affect a hearing problem. This can be very effective when answering telephone calls from your descendants... Ask 'Who is it?' at least twice (as if you don't recognise your own child or grandchild's voice) and 'Can you repeat that?' should be bellowed at regular intervals. Cultivate the air of being confused. Buy a hearing aid, switch it on but don't let it sit properly in your ear: everyone else will hear an increasingly irritating high-pitched whine while you, on the other hand, won't.*

Criticism/Observations

- *Never appear happy; grandparents carry the burden of advanced age on their shoulders. This is emphasised by constantly referring to the Good Old Days, saying things like 'Wouldn't have happened in my day' and generally seeming as though the world and modern attitudes are completely beyond your comprehension.*

How to be a GHASTLY GRANDPARENT

Reliability

- *Never, ever, be punctual. Make a point of turning up a week early or a day late. Likewise, never be ready to leave when someone comes to collect you in their car. It's expected.*

- *Cultivate a vague attitude and general absent-mindedness. However, always make a point of remembering every birthday in the family, without fail. Send a card plus a small gift, and call each person on their special day. The 'small' gift should be*

...and have fun!

an inexpensive, useful item (socks or gloves, or a wooden toy or puzzle), preferably hand-made for that personal, penny-pinching touch.

- *No one will remember your own birthday with any consistency, so your diligence will be an uncomfortable plus in your favour as you tread an uneasy line between being obnoxious and lovable.*

Over-Indulgence

- *When attending a family meal (not, it goes*

without saying, in your own home), eat very little before arriving. Then eat everything that's put in front of you and pinch forkfuls of food from other plates. Ask for seconds (and thirds, and fourths). Drink to the point of, but not beyond, excess, especially if you're not paying. Take a doggy bag if eating in a posh restaurant and make sure you fill it, even if it means drifting around non-family tables for odd scraps.

Home Presentation

- *Maintain an air of untidiness in rooms*

...and have fun!

likely to be seen by your family, especially the kitchen. Keep a few cans/jars/tubs of mouldy, out-of-date food lying around, and your fridge should appear almost empty.

- *Allow dust to accumulate. Why should you keep the place clean and tidy just for them, when their guilt will drive them to spring clean for you? The same goes for the garden, which has become such a burden for you to manage, particularly since your arm/back/neck/leg keeps playing up.*

Leisure Pursuits

- *Keep these secret from your family whenever possible. Crown Green Bowling or tennis on a regular basis is unlikely to square with your bad arm/back/leg, is it? Be sensible. Such energetic activities won't be a problem if your family lives some distance away, but even then you shouldn't display your latest trophies in the china cabinet or leave newspaper reports of your sporting prowess lying around.*

...and have fun!

Technophobia

- *Modern gadgets, like MP3 players, Gameboys, mobile phones with irritating ring tones and even computers are devices created by the Devil so that the ignorant or lazy can while away the day and cause extreme annoyance to those who wish to lead a proper life.*

- *Keep your gadgets hidden away and never profess knowledge or pass any comment which would imply interest. Ban family from bringing modern gadgets into your house, purely in retaliation for not being allowed to smoke like a chimney in theirs.*

Driving Techniques

- *Crunch the gears; peer short-sightedly through the windscreen; be cautiously deliberate at all times; never proceed at more than 20 mph on streets or 50 mph on motorways; brake repeatedly; always wear a seat belt, even when stationary.*

- *Buy a bright yellow steering lock and make a point of checking each door is locked even*

...and have fun!

if you have a central locking system.

- *Consider wearing a cyclist's crash helmet inside the car ('You can't be too careful'). Make your son/daughter pay for petrol ('Oh, dear, I forgot my wallet/purse again'), particularly when the tank is almost empty.*

Bear in mind these are just guidelines. Advancing age will inevitably give rise to additional situations, each of which you should exploit to the full.

How to be a GHASTLY GRANDPARENT

Don't overuse specific quirks, nor adopt them concurrently or in rapid succession. Drip them into your life one by one, and vary their frequency.

The best way to achieve success is to prepare a spreadsheet or schedule on your non-existent computer, with features listed on the left and corresponding date boxes alongside. Then, all you need to do is enter the date upon which you last used each feature so that you can keep track of your behaviour. You could also enter the date in

...and have fun!

bold text whenever a reaction has been particularly effective. You will, of course, be able to add to the list as time passes. Some signs of ageing will pop up without warning and at the most inconvenient times; don't be worried, just add them to the list. Cultivation is the key.

Aim to activate all quirks over a period of at least 20 years and aim to call a halt when your youngest grandchild has left home. If he or she seems unlikely ever to fly the family nest, consider offering a financial bribe to speed up the process... or be prepared to carry on indefinitely.

Once the period of Self-protection By Subterfuge is no longer necessary, you should (unless nature dictates otherwise) put an end to all unreasonable and downright disgusting habits. The rest of your life should be one of good behaviour and general bonhomie, where members of the family will be only too happy to welcome your company and do anything for you. This is essential to your future well-being... there

...and have fun!

will come a time when you really will need their help. You won't be healthy and self-sufficient forever. On the other hand, if you're unlucky enough to become a great-grandparent, you may need to reconsider your position, but only to a certain extent. No one in their right mind is going to ask a great-grandparent to baby-sit or provide (shaky) hands-on help, so you may be able to get away with observing (with increasing amusement) as your children try to work out how you managed to get away with so much for so long. It's up to them whether

How to be a GHASTLY GRANDPARENT

they have the courage to take your advice...

if you can be bothered to give it, of course.

Grand Babies and Infants

How to be a GHASTLY GRANDPARENT

He, she or it has arrived (possibly even 'they'!)... your first grandchild in the form of a mini Winston Churchill (fortunately without the cigar or 'V' sign, at least for the present).

The grandbaby is concentrating on developing powerful lungs, processing mushy food and generating unpleasant scents and milky puke. Now is when you need to spend some time in the quiet and comfort of your own home.

...and have fun!

Glad though you may be to have another generation to continue the family line, babies are smelly, noisy and inconvenient. They take a lot of looking after. You don't want to be involved with all that hassle again, do you? Oh, no. Resist any request to baby-sit for a few hours to give mum and dad a break. Develop a chesty cough or hoarse voice. Say you appear to have broken out in a rash and don't want to harm the child. Wrap your fingers in bandages, saying that you had an accident with a chain saw and won't be able to change nappies. Better

How to be a GHASTLY GRANDPARENT

still; go on a cheap SAGA holiday to Benidorm for three months. Before you depart, thoughtfully give mum a few balls of wool and a couple of 1940s clothes patterns to go with the needles you donated earlier. Present the new dad with another *Playboy* magazine, two tubes of KY gel, ear plugs and a sleeping potion.

Things will have improved by the time you return. However, mum will be champing at the bit to return to work. This is the time you should become actively involved with a

...and have fun!

voluntary organisation, preferably one for widows or widowers with young children of their own to rear. Guilt will quash any thoughts of asking you to undertake long-term childminding except in desperation.

Doesn't time fly? Before you know it, the smelly bundle of powerless grandbaby will transform itself into a snivelling wretch prone to having tantrums. What's worse, it can now walk but, with a bit of luck, should be potty trained.

How to be a GHASTLY GRANDPARENT

If he/she/it/they come to visit, move every valuable ornament from high shelves and glass-fronted cabinets to convenient locations well within a child's reach. One (ornament, not child) is bound to get broken; more than one is a bonus. The fact that these were family heirlooms/valuable antiques will only add to extreme feelings of guilt and will deter future forays into your safe haven for a year or two.

Make a note of the date each grandchild last visited… it will come in useful some

...and have fun!

time in the future when you'll be able to say, accusingly, 'I hardly ever get a visit.' More guilt.

It's important for your own future welfare and peace of mind to ensure you give your grandchild love and affection... but you must never show it in front of the parents. Wait until they're out of the room. This is extremely important. The parents will be convinced you don't care but the children, as they get older, will be able to add it to their arsenal of arguments against their

How to be a GHASTLY GRANDPARENT

parents. What goes around…

As you know from your own experience, infants transform into children alarmingly quickly. Grandchildren can be both very charming and highly entertaining but this is the time when you should be most on your guard.

Visits from grandchildren should be affairs lasting no more than an hour or two and certainly not overnight. Any longer than a couple of hours implies that you're not

...and have fun!

averse to long-term childcare, a view that should be nipped in the bud at the first opportunity. You have so many commitments elsewhere that it simply isn't possible to include regular childminding. By sticking to your guns, a visit from your grandchildren will be an event both you and they will cherish. At least until they get older.

Become actively involved with your grandchildren by doing things together: simple baking, making toys from cardboard and paper, etc. Don't do anything dangerous.

How to be a GHASTLY GRANDPARENT

Better still, get them involved in tidying up and cleaning (which they certainly won't do at home) and resist all temptation to let them watch television or play computer games. Talk to them, preferably about The Old Days (their parents won't be the least interested in your past but it's important that you try to gain your grandchildren's attention early on) to give them a sense of belonging to an old, established and respectable family.

In short, do all you can to make friends

...and have fun!

with the youngsters while at the same time brainwashing them in whatever rules or beliefs you hold dear: these are bound to conflict with their parents' opinions. Close understanding now will pay dividends later.

School events present a not-to-be-missed opportunity to get revenge for the way your own children treated you when they were the same age as your grandchildren. It's payback time!

How to be a **GHASTLY GRANDPARENT**

Your prime objective is to show the world how off-hand your children treat you and that life with them is not a wonderful experience. The most obvious way of achieving this is to give the impression that you're neglected and unloved.

Begin by wearing old, tatty clothes, the smellier the better (put a moth ball in every pocket and spray yourself liberally with Old Spice aftershave or English Lavender perfume) but not so grubby that they look as though they're more suitable for

...and have fun!

gardening. Do not clean your shoes.

If you're a man, don't shave that morning or, if you do, miss a few areas. Cultivate ear and nasal hair to the point where it could be made into plaits. Wear mismatched socks or none at all.

If you're a woman, mess up your hair and wear just one earring. Keep a grubby handkerchief with obvious signs of use tucked into, but hanging from, the cuff of your sleeve. Make sure your tights

How to be a **GHASTLY GRANDPARENT**

have a prominent hole in them, plus at least one badly-darned hole. In no circumstances should you dress like a tart; fishnet stockings, low-cut blouse, mini skirt and high heeled shoes will not give the right impression, even if you would like to flirt with anyone wearing trousers (or a dress, for that matter).

Occasionally rub a non-existent ache in your lower back, forearm, or upper leg. Wince now and again. If anyone enquires, say you're not as young as you used to be and that you do the gardening or carry heavy shopping. But don't complain. Just sigh and shake your head sadly while wiping your eyes or nose with your dirty hanky.

Take a camera/camcorder to film the event. Other parents will be convinced you're a pervert, so be prepared to say your son/daughter insisted on you bringing it when a scowling teacher approaches. Blame will shift from you, and the school will keep a jaundiced yet protective eye on your grandchildren for the rest of their academic

How to be a GHASTLY GRANDPARENT

lives. Not every pupil gets that sort of attention, so you'll be doing them a favour.

It will help if your grandchild sports a bruise on their arm/leg/eye. If one is absent, somehow put a spot of permanent blue/black Quink ink and bright yellow iodine on their skin and rub it off with your all-purpose hanky and a dribble of spit. The resulting stain will be quite convincing. Wait patiently for the opportunity to mention casually that the child is accident-prone. Apparently. Furthermore, since

...and have fun!

children tend to run straight to their grandparents rather than parents after an event, suspicion of parental mistreatment will be greatly heightened.

Should anyone express concern at your health/well-being, be shrewdly non-judgmental. Say something like, 'Well, you know how it is, they're very busy parents. I'm sure they do their best.'

With a bit of luck, someone may send you a food parcel anonymously, or you'll find

How to be a GHASTLY GRANDPARENT

your name on a list of pensioners receiving Harvest Festival and Christmas hampers from the local church.

Grand Children

How to be a GHASTLY GRANDPARENT

The few years of transition between infancy and childhood pass very quickly and, before you know it, your grandchildren will have all the appearance of being real human beings capable of thought. They will also become increasingly inquisitive, noisy and irritating.

Their parents won't have a clue how to cope. This is where your own powers and experience will help shape their character. With patience and persistence, you'll be able to put right their parents' shortcomings.

...and have fun!

And emphasise their inadequacy. This is not to say you abandon all efforts to remain smugly aloof from becoming involved in the day-to-day process of rearing them. Quite the contrary. You have to strike a balance between seeming incompetent, mentally deranged and prone to alcoholism, and the desire to exert some influence over and have fun with your grandchildren.

After having spent the first few years of their lives discouraging visits to your home, leap at the first opportunity to look after

How to be a **GHASTLY GRANDPARENT**

them ('Just for a few hours, mind') when they have reached the stage where you think it might be a happy experience. Their parents, shell-shocked and almost speechless at this sudden change, will suffer considerable mental anguish before they reluctantly agree. Fix a definite date and time and, for once, don't forget it.

The first solo visit by a grandchild is the most important. You must get everything right, and leave nothing to chance. Remember, this is the real beginning of

...and have fun!

their lives and everything you do now could have long term consequences affecting comfort in your twilight years.

Your main objective must be to mould their characters in a way that you failed to do with your own children. It's a well known fact that family members from adjacent generations never get on but descendants from subsequent generations will get on with you like a house on fire. Why is this? Simply because the role of children is to make their parents suffer. That's all that's

How to be a GHASTLY GRANDPARENT

meant by the phrase 'The Generation Gap' which only applies to parent/child relationships. It doesn't affect grandparents/grandchildren.

So take advantage of the situation. Always remember that your involvement is only for a few hours at a time, and not on a regular basis (make that very clear from the onset or you'll soon become a frequent childminder). OK, so you'll feel knackered at the end of each session but you'll have the satisfaction of knowing that you've

...and have fun!

helped mould a decent human being... unlike those prats of children you reared without proper help from your own parents.

Why should you suddenly have this change of heart? Because it will ultimately cause more friction and disagreement between your children and grandchildren. The Generation Gap syndrome needs your help if it is going to continue. The simple truth is that, if you have behaved improperly until now, your children will regard you with

How to be a **GHASTLY GRANDPARENT**

deep suspicion and despair (yet they still love you, preferably from a distance). By doing the right things with your grandchildren, the latter will love you without question and regard their own parents with suspicion and despair.

So, take the time and trouble to make each visit to your home, well away from parental interference, a happy and worthwhile experience. But how do you do this without compromising your previous actions? By drawing a distinction between your home

...and have fun!

life and the life you lead when in your children's company. Simple, really.

First of all, continue to uphold the rules you set earlier. No MP3 players, mobile phones or hand-held games contraptions. Kids only have them because their parents caved in to peer pressure and 'anything for a quiet life'. You don't have that problem. 'In loco parentis' doesn't mean you have to be weak-willed or suffer accordingly.

Confiscate any gadgets that are smuggled in

How to be a GHASTLY GRANDPARENT

(you may want to sit on the toilet and try them out without your grandchildren knowing). You could also sabotage them if you feel so inclined... like changing the batteries for flat ones, using a Stanley knife to almost sever headphone cables which will break after you've returned them, etc. The point of this exercise is that you won't suffer the constant 'Tsh! Tsh!' noise from the MP3 players and mobile phones, and the game machines won't work. With little else to occupy their time, your grandchildren's full attention will turn to you.

...and have fun!

Children, whether they know it or not, survive on three things and it's as well for you to bear these in mind at all times: food, busy hands and occupied minds. A fourth thing, sleep, is a bonus but perhaps you shouldn't encourage it during the visit.

- *Food*

    This can present problems to the unwary grandparent who may well enjoy the fat-laden junk food dispensed to the grandchildren on a regular basis by their parents. To emphasise the difference in a show of worrying about their health, hide anything that smacks of convenience food. Stock up with carrots and fresh fruit, all of which are good for nibbling on and remove the need to waste time doing real cooking, which won't be appreciated anyway. Perhaps (if you're feeling particularly vindictive) make baked beans on granary toast a favourite; the effects should start to kick in just as their parents come to collect them in the car...

...and have fun!

- *Busy Hands*

To begin with, continue to let them do your washing and washing up, clean the house and take pride in making the place spotless. As they get older, let them carry your shopping or do a little hard digging in the garden. Make out you're slow and tired because a) they'll feel sympathetic and b) it'll give them a sense of achievement. As their parents have long since given up any hope of getting their kids to do anything around the house, all this will have a distinct novelty value.

How to be a GHASTLY GRANDPARENT

To vary the 'Busy Hands' diet, invest in a few colouring books, stiff card and crayons (but avoid the temptation to buy paint boxes, which always create a mess) to keep them quietly occupied on rainy days (or at any other time, for that matter). Approaching birthdays or Christmas provide opportunities for them to create cards for their parents.

If they show any real talent, consider having the cards printed professionally: you'll be able to sell them for a small profit at the corner shop or next church

...and have fun!

fayre, or you could save money by not having to buy nondescript commercially produced cards.

Continue to make things together, or embark on more advanced baking and cooking. Time always flies by when you're being creative and, unless you become heavily involved in carpentry, home decorating or relaying slabs on the patio, it does not have to be too energetic. On the other hand, don't underestimate a child's enthusiasm to participate in domestic activities outside their home environment, however ambitious the project. Just imagine the look on their parents' faces when they find out!

Don't be tempted to help with their homework, although there's no reason why you shouldn't apart from the fact that teaching methods aren't so effective and are infinitely more confusing than they were in your schooldays. A better idea is to invent projects which require them to work out maths problems or send them on a search for information. Schools, teachers and parents may be

...and have fun!

failing them as a matter of course and this is your chance to repair some of the damage. Learning how to find information and applying mathematical principles to every day situations is much easier to teach in a home environment.

- *Occupied Minds*

Keeping your grandchild's hands busy doesn't always mean their minds are fully occupied. Kneading dough for four hundred bread rolls for the Pensioners' Party you're holding tomorrow is a

How to be a GHASTLY GRANDPARENT

routine job. Talking is a good way of taking their tiny minds off how long the work will take. Clever, eh?

Odd events from family history are a good fallback. As you will have noticed, your own children weren't the least interested in your past, but grandchildren are a different kettle of fish entirely. What you got up to as a child of their age will intrigue them to the point of mouths dropping open in astonishment. You came from a different world, planet even. And that's not all: once you start regaling

...and have fun!

them with tales of your own parents, grand- and great-grandparents, you're delving not into another planet but a different universe. Every family has a history; every family has its fair share of weirdos. Remember great-aunt Hildegard who ran off with a Chinaman and the scandal it caused? And great-great-grandfather Ebenezer who fought off four thousand head-hunting pygmies single handed? ('That's his head on the ground in that photo.')

They'll not just be intrigued, they'll

How to be a **GHASTLY GRANDPARENT**

develop insatiable appetites for more. Just remember how young they are... keep the really lurid stuff for when they're in their teens, when holding their interest will be much more difficult. The important thing is to create interest, and engender a feeling that you're treating them as a confidant rather than a child.

Make the most of the time spent alone with your grandchildren... it won't be long before they become unruly, miserable teenagers with enormous chips on their shoulders and an overpowering sense of

...and have fun!

parental victimisation. Which presents you with yet another opportunity to get your own back on their parents...

Grand Teenagers

...and have fun!

Looking back, what should you have done, as the parent of a recalcitrant teenager, when you had the chance? Should you have kept them confined to their bedroom? Should you have shown them the back of your hand more frequently? Whatever you'd have liked to have done, you were the unwitting victim of standard teenage behaviour. You'd been just the same once, shown similar disrespect, worn the same t-shirt, although you wouldn't dare admit it.

No, your limited powers as a parent were

How to be a **GHASTLY GRANDPARENT**

eroded beyond redemption by Modern Thinking, rampant do-gooders whose mean, suspicious minds viewed every attempt at discipline or parental control as the act of perverts or sadistic minds. In short, you failed. Where did you go wrong? Or, more to the point, why do teenage renegades get on so well with their farting, poverty-stricken, obnoxious grandparents? Because the old fogies set, and adhere to, ground rules. Because they treat the grandteenagers as human beings, not some money-swallowing bottomless pit. Because they

...and have fun!

give them the time of day. Because they exercise cunning to exploit the Generation Gap while the parents are too busy fire-fighting family flare-ups... Parents just don't stand a chance.

But what should you, as the grandparent of a teenager affected by hormones developing at their own uncontrolled pace, do now? You don't relish the prospect of handling the increasingly wide range of adolescent problems arising on a daily basis, but you do want the endless misery suffered by their

How to be a GHASTLY GRANDPARENT

parents to continue without appearing to take sides or add fuel to the fire.

The best thing to do is to carry on as before. Watch your grandchild closely to see if there are topics of particular interest. Not every teenager is obsessed with pop music, senseless mobile phone calls to their friends every minute of the waking day, or sitting glued to the television for hours at a time.

Away from their parents' critical eyes, teenagers can be quite normal. Well, for

...and have fun!

some of the time. If they seem troubled, ask discreet questions until you get to the real cause. It may be that running out of credit on the mobile phone, frustrating as it is, hides the fact that their true love has eluded them. Matters of the heart will be uppermost in their minds during these confusing years. All their troubles will be related to Love, one way or another. Their school work will be suffering, their parents will be far too repressive, their mates will seem hellbent on causing trouble and trying every trick in the peer-pressure book to make your cherished grandchild follow their lead and fall off the rails.

Teenagers, essentially, are children but with one major difference. They are now approaching adulthood. OK, so they're nowhere near as mature as you were at their age (dream on!) and life is a great deal easier for them than it ever was for you... or is it? The pressures of modern life demand quick answers to everything, not like in your day when there weren't so many distractions. Money, a scarce commodity forty years ago,

...and have fun!

is made available to all and sundry without any regard for how it is to be repaid. Consideration is seldom given to actually waiting, Heaven forbid, until you have saved up to buy something. If it were, far less would be spent on eye-catching or so-called 'must-have' rubbish.

Your role as a grandparent must be to hold a steady handle on the tiller or, put another way, provide an unruffled, calm approach when confronted with Life's little problems, including teenagers. This is the period in their lives when an hour's reasoned, non-judgmental conversation will have them eating out of your hands. And, from their parents' point of view, nothing could cast greater aspersions on their child-rearing abilities than their kids actually going to visit their grandparents willingly, if only for a brief period, to get away from the constant nagging.

A short time in an anguish-free environment is all teenagers often want or need, and the effort you invest over the last few trouble-

...and have fun!

free years will be well rewarded later on. They'll know what to expect in your sanctuary, they'll understand the rules and appreciate that it's a waste of time asking you to buy the latest CD by the current talentless, mindless celebrity nobody.

Talking and listening are your main weapons now, unless you really want to get involved in a lengthy, challenging do-it-yourself project or help re-phrase the latest heart-rending love 'text' message (handwritten love letter, in your day).

How to be a GHASTLY GRANDPARENT

This is the time when the seedier, meaty and infinitely more flavoursome Tales From The Family Tree will come in useful. But resist the temptation to make them more lurid and sensual than they really were. Always tell the truth, whatever the subject... unwanted pregnancies, criminal activities and wartime exploits are always top favourites. And certainly don't be slow in hinting at their parents' misdemeanours... just enough to provoke interest so that they can seek further embarrassing details from the parents themselves. Or come back to

...and have fun!

you for more. If nothing else, it'll take their minds off their current problems. Their parents should be grateful. They won't be, but they should be. And for once in their short lives, your grandchildren may look at their parents through different eyes. Then again, they may not. Either way, you win.

But even the best laid plans have a habit of falling flat on their faces. Not all cunningly conceived schemes are destined to succeed, regardless of the effort involved. How do you react if your teenage grandchildren

How to be a GHASTLY GRANDPARENT

treat you with the same lack of appreciation or respect as they do their parents? The answer is obvious: if they behave like children, treat them like children... with knobs on. If a quiet chat explaining the effects their behaviour is having on your relationship doesn't yield a good result, take drastic action. Send them a very childish card and gift for their birthday and Christmas... something so obviously insulting that they'll either take extreme umbrage or, more likely, appreciate the subtlety. Don't go overboard: a baby's

...and have fun!

dummy is perhaps a little over the top but a baby doll which wets itself or an action man is a good starting point... whether you give the doll to a boy or an action man to a girl is entirely up to you and the message you wish to convey... you may have spotted behavioural problems their parents prefer to ignore, hoping they'll go away.

If that doesn't work, then Hell mend them. Do the same to them as you've been doing to their parents while they were mere embryos. It could be fun. And they won't

How to be a GHASTLY GRANDPARENT

know what hit them.

Grand Adults

How to be a GHASTLY GRANDPARENT

Your grandchildren have grown up. They've finished school or university and are now taking their first tentative steps into the big, wide world. How twisted or mentally unstable they've become as a direct result of your connivance is not your problem.

You've managed to keep in touch by telephone, letter, greetings card and occasional (increasingly occasional!) visits. You seem to be on very good terms with them, a fact which continues to confound their parents to the point where your

...and have fun!

outrageous behaviour (to them, at least) is almost tolerated. But the time will come when communication with your grandchildren becomes less frequent. They may move away further than you'd like but it's their life, not yours.

Mass-produced birthday and, if you're lucky, Christmas cards are bought reluctantly from Smith's or from the cheap stall at the market and contain nothing more than a hastily scribbled, barely decipherable signature. No enquiry as to your health or a brief note on what's been happening at their end. If you're not careful, memory of you will be consigned to oblivion.

What should you do in these circumstances? Make every effort to keep in touch, that's what! Telephone them regularly and leave messages when they're out. Send postcards whenever you go on holiday. Write letters posing questions which require a reply; if none is forthcoming, send a follow-up note enclosing a stamped, self-addressed envelope expressing concern at their apparent poverty

...and have fun!

and apologise profusely for interrupting their busy schedules (people don't have 'lives' any more, just 'schedules' and 'lifestyles'. What nonsense!)...

Persistence will eventually do the trick, as far as keeping in touch with you is concerned. As for their parents, well, remember how your very existence took a back seat when your own children began their careers and hunted for a life partner (not 'husband' or 'wife', note) to provide social companionship? With luck, they'll have forgotten the trials

How to be a **GHASTLY GRANDPARENT**

and tribulations of coping with teenagers and the heavy financial demands of students. Now they'll be fending off requests for cash, either to buy that essential top-of-the-range car or for a down payment on a mortgage, both of which (and sometimes more) inevitably arise when their child makes contact for the first time in months. And the parents will wonder why it is that you know more about what their children have been doing, and what their long term plans are, than they do.

...and have fun!

Furthermore, if you find yourself in that increasingly common rank of great-grandparents, you'll be able to take a rear seat while your children assume the role of grandparents. They may even approach you for advice willingly, in which case refer them to this book. It'll open their eyes wider than those of a rabbit caught in a car's headlights in the pitch black of night on a lonely country road. And they'll respect you all the more for it.

Grand Decline,
or Where There's
a Will...

...and have fun!

You are, like all members of the human race, not immortal. Shame, really. When you eventually shuffle off this mortal coil, pop your clogs or kick the bucket, all the knowledge and wisdom you have accumulated over many years will be lost forever. Does it matter? Probably not. But your reputation and behaviour will be the talking point for generations to come, so your memory, if nothing else, will live on.

Getting old is, generally, not a pleasant experience. Everything, both physical and

How to be a GHASTLY GRANDPARENT

mental, begins to fall apart. OK, your family has already had some experience of dealing with your shocking behaviour (if you've followed the advice given in these pages), but now it's for real. You may be one of the lucky ones, where your descendants have been trained to regard you with at least a modicum of affection despite your quirky ways. On the other hand, you're probably not, so now's the time to dangle carrots rather than wield cudgels to get your own way.

...and have fun!

Take good care of yourself... the last thing you want is to be slipped quietly into a nursing home or protected dwelling for the elderly. Keep your mind and body active so that, as far as possible, you can survive on your own. Having said that, you'll probably want to enlist the help of your family to do the more unpleasant and strenuous work, like washing, gardening and cleaning.

Your main weapon now becomes your Last Will and Testament. Drop subtle hints that, although your home is too big to manage on

How to be a GHASTLY GRANDPARENT

your own, it's now worth somewhere in the region of half a million. And that doesn't include the small fortune you've accumulated by scrimping and saving over the years. That should get your family interested. Ask your children and grandchildren for advice on what should go in the Will. They'll try to appear fair and reasonable but you know they'll each want the lion's share.

Now's the time you could gently suggest someone helps out on a regular basis, albeit for a few hours a week. Perhaps on a rota,

...and have fun!

which would involve all your descendants. If they bite, you'll have the distinct satisfaction of having each and every one of them at your beck and call... for as long as it takes. You won't be here forever and you really must visit the solicitor at the earliest opportunity, 'just in case'. When each one visits to do their reluctant stint with a happy smile, ask if there's anything they'd like to have when you die: ornaments, your trophies, your collection of tobacco tins or embroidery silks.

How to be a **GHASTLY GRANDPARENT**

The word 'die' can have a remarkable effect on some people. You may be fit and hearty, you may have another twenty years of active life ahead of you (don't forget to keep up the pretence of aches, pains and forgetfulness), but they will expect an imminent departure once you mention the 'D' word. So, slip it into conversation during each visit, just to keep the thought alive.

It's extremely important for you to keep in touch with everyone, in addition to

...and have fun!

when they arrive for this week's chores. Enclose personal, handwritten letters in birthday and Christmas cards saying how much you love them, how happy you are to have had them as part of your life, that you couldn't have wished for a better son/daughter/grandchild, etc. This will not only have tears flowing like mountain streams, it will heighten their sense of guilt and enhance feelings of personal responsibility for your welfare.

However, all this leaves the question of

How to be a GHASTLY GRANDPARENT

your Last Will and Testament… You could dispense with a will altogether, which will result in bickering and ill-feeling between your beneficiaries. But is that fair on them, and should you, after years of careful connivance, relinquish control and leave the decisions to someone else? No. Absolutely not.

You could leave your estate in trust for your grandchildren, thus annoying your children, who have been borrowing heavily on the understanding that your estate will

...and have fun!

see them right.

You could bequeath everything to a cats and dogs home, thus adding irritation and expense when your children contest the will and question your sanity when you made it.

You could leave everything to be divided equally between your surviving children, but that's not very imaginative, is it? Not unless you've re-mortgaged your house and spent virtually every penny of your life

How to be a GHASTLY GRANDPARENT

savings having a Good Time in your twilight years. By the time the building society or bank has taken its exorbitant share of the net proceeds, there'll be precious little left. Worth considering, eh? And you'll be able to see the disappointment from the comfort of your very own Heavenly cloud.

Grand Exit

How to be a GHASTLY GRANDPARENT

The greatest contribution you can make to your family is dying in style. Do your utmost to make it an outstanding event, preferably a sudden one so that it catches them totally unprepared. Yes, by now they should be expecting your demise but, having waited in lip-biting anticipation for over twenty years, a sudden exit will catch them all off their guard.

Why not take up a dangerous sport? The insurance companies, scavengers that they are (and far more devious than you could

...and have fun!

ever be to avoid paying out), will have lost interest in you as a safe investment long ago. Snowboarding on the Matterhorn, paragliding in the Andes, mountaineering without ropes in the Alps... the opportunities are endless. Whatever you decide, make it legal. Foolhardy, but legal. Circumnavigating the M25 on a unicycle against the flow of traffic is no more than an act of stupidity and you will gain neither respect nor sympathy. Extreme sports are much more exciting and romantic.

How to be a GHASTLY GRANDPARENT

But however Fate dictates you will expire, try and make it happen on a Memorable Day, like Christmas, Boxing or New Year's Day. Then you'll have the otherworldly satisfaction of knowing you'll never be forgotten... with the added bonus that you'll make everyone's life a misery for years to come.

Immortality at last!

And Finally...

How to be a GHASTLY GRANDPARENT

If you really believe that excellent relationships with your children and grandchildren are of the utmost importance to your welfare, ignore the advice given in this book. However, you may be proud of the results achieved by long-term deception, and may have absolutely no desire to relinquish control after so long in the driving seat and pulling the strings in your very own personal puppet theatre. Even the most powerful dictators never know when to stop, and usually come to a sticky end. Do you want that to happen to you? Probably

...and have fun!

not. Loneliness comes as standard with Old Age and, after due consideration, you may reach the conclusion that being used, fleeced and losing control of your life is better than the alternatives.

You have been warned!

Oh!... and don't forget to bequeath this book in your Last Will and Testament!

The World's Funniest Proverbs

JAMES ALEXANDER

Beauty is in the eye of the beer holder

Don't take life too seriously - it's not permanent

Multi-tasking: the art of screwing up everything all at once

Never marry for money; you will borrow cheaper

ISBN: 978-1-906051-07-5, £5.99, hb

HOW TO BE A HAPPY OLD MAN

a little guide for grumpy old men

George Evans

ISBN 978-1-906051-11-2, £5.99, hb

www.crombiejardine.com